Reflections

"I love Lisa's authentic stories of the impact her Granny had on her life. She shares firsthand the importance and impact family has in shaping us all. A great gift for all generations."

- ANGELA AHRENDTS DBE,
Former SVP Apple Retail, CEO Burberry

"Granny is officially the OG, the GOAT! Lisa is right behind her with her ability to document Granny's wit over the decades and tell her story with such candor, empathy, lightheartedness, and respect. Granny would be proud of Lisa for capturing the essence of their family dynamics. I still laugh aloud every time I think about the chicken grease story!"

CYNTHIA JOHNSON,
Community Development Specialist,
NAACP Medgar Evers Award Recipient

"Just Keep Living" is a priceless gem. I laughed the entire time - enjoying the anecdotes and antics between Lisa and her Granny. This book is a reminder for all of us to slow down and cherish the moments we have with our loved ones as they give us the strength and wisdom to carry on. This is a book you'll want to keep handy when you're having a bad day. In less than 2 minutes, you'll be laughing with unbridled joy. And like Granny, I'm not 369 on that piece of advice!"

- KEITH POWELL,
Fortune 500 and Non-profit Executive,
C-CRETS Podcast Host

"Grandmother's speak words from God that water generations. Lisa has captured these pearls of wisdom that feed the soul, warm and stir the heart!"
-TRACY P. JOHNSON PHD,
Associate Vice Chancellor, Student Wellness and Support

"Just Keep Living" offers a refreshing pause from the frenetic task of navigating through the complexities of today's society. As I firmly believe there's "genius in simplicity", I found Granny's quips to be simultaneously profound, enlightening, insightful, wise, and humorous. Only a genius can pack so much into so few words!! Regardless of one's perspective on today's political, religious, and social issues, anyone who reads this book is guaranteed to glean fresh insights.

Beneath the various points of view and perspectives, "Just Keep Living" is underpinned by a heart-warming core theme of multi-generational familial love. "Just Keep Living" is a reminder for all to prioritize and cherish time with loved ones as tomorrow isn't promised to any of us."
- REGGIE COLBY,
Vice President, Supply Chain/Manufacturing

"There are conversations that are priceless. They just can not be invented. JUST KEEP LIVING took me on a journey of laughter, pause, and sweet reflections of my own grandparents. Having the opportunity to experience Granny in real time, I am certain that as you read 'Just Keep Living', she will become part of your family. You can't get ready for what you are about to read. Oh, and I totally get the story about the Greens!"
SANDRA MOSLEY,
Financial Coach, Author

Just
Keep
Living

Just
Keep
Living

Conversations with Granny

LISA M. BENNETT
& JESSIE M. WILSON

Naked
Truth
PUBLISHING

Lead Editor: Kori Walker
Editor: Cynthia Johnson
Book Cover and Design: Daniel Ojedokun
Website Design: Suraj Gupta

Library of Congress Cataloging-in-Publication Data has been applied for.
Just Keep Living (paperback) 978-1-7378196-0-8
Just Keep Living (Ebook) 978-1-7378196-1-5

Printed in the United States of America

Naked
Truth
PUBLISHING

Dedication

This book is dedicated to my grandparents:

Jessie M. Wilson aka "Granny"
JP Wallace aka "Granddad"
Mattie Lee Perdue-Wallace aka "Grandma Mattie"
Queen E. Taylor aka "Grandma"
Richard Bass aka "Poppa"
Idella Bass aka "Grandma Idella"
Guy Robinson aka "Pop"

It is the sum of you that created me.

Table of Contents

Introduction

Blessed!

This is the word that comes to mind. There is an old church song that says, "When I look back over my life and I think things over. I can truly say that I've been blessed." That is MY TESTIMONY!

I grew up in a multi-generational family (no less than 5 generations at any given time). I had my mom and her siblings, my grandparents and their siblings, my great grandparents and their siblings, as well as all of the offspring. I am now 55. My parents and some of my grandparents have transitioned. However, there are still 2 generations of my family that are older than me and at least 2 generations that are younger than me. I don't know any other way to describe it except to say 'blessed'!

As you might imagine, there are lots of family stories that could be told or written. While there is great joy in the longevity of my blood line, it also hits very hard when there is a loss. We are never prepared to say goodbye.

My mom's passing was particularly difficult for me. She died "out of order" or out of succession. In my family, most people died because they were 90+ years old. It is rare for us to have a death for any other reason.

I desperately needed to find a way to cope with losing my mom and also her younger sister within months of each other. To heal, I decided to spend more time with my grandparents. I wanted to make sure they were "ok" with our new lives and I desperately wanted to be "ok" too. I made a commitment to celebrate them more often, spend more physical time, and talk with them more often. After all, we were each other's reminders of my mom. They saw glimpses of my mom in me, I saw glimpses of her in them, and how they each had a fingerprint on who she was and who I am still becoming. In this period, it seems that I started to hear my grandparents' voices differently. As I listened to them more, I became aware of their natural comedic and wise views on life. I started sharing some of our interactions on social media. After a few stories, I received LOTS of positive feedback. I unknowingly found a small, but captive audience of readers who enjoyed my recounts of crazy conversations with my grandparents. People actually looked forward to my postings. They were inspired by the refreshing, wise, no-nonsense of these "old" people. My Granny, in particular, had a way of dissecting the most complex topics into simple straightforward, unfiltered responses! Her day to day antics, wisdom, and her philosophical response to every inquiry, "Just Keep Living", helped me hold onto my joy.

So, I hope this small collection of short anecdotes and conversations with Granny will inspire you to laugh out loud.

Granny offered a lot of commentary that seemed entertaining and 'passe' on the surface, but 90% of the time it carried a much deeper meaning and conversation. I will explore those aspects in another book.

This book is not about any particular story, situation, or lesson. It's about my everyday walk with my Granny. There was no topic that was off limits to her. She discussed religion, race, love, sex, politics, sports, music, tv shows, movies... anything.   She asked questions about everything. She ALWAYS had an opinion and you would CERTAINLY walk away with more to think about than you bargained for. There is no rhythm or rhyme to the stories I am sharing with you today. They simply provide peace, love, laughter, and comfort to me when I am missing her. I pray my reminiscing brings some joy and perhaps keeps you close to your grandparents. The gift of their wisdom and life's experiences are beyond measure.

Often, Granny's stoic demeanor can make me recall the opening passage of the Tales of Two Cities by Dickens. "It was the best of times and the worst of times." But it seems, no matter what time is at hand, Granny's faith and humor never fail her.

The worst of times for me was immediately surrounding my mother's passing. Unless you experience it, there really are no words or any other thing that can prepare you for it. So first, I pray that your mom is still with you. Enjoy every moment. Dare I say, even cherish every fight, argument, and disagreement. There is no one who can love you more. If your mom has transitioned, remember, you are not alone. I hope you will be able to laugh.

Granny and I are just sitting around having a casual conversation and the phone rings.

Me: Hello. I am sorry. I have told you several times that my mom is deceased. Please stop calling, she obviously will not be renewing her service.

Granny: Lisa, who is that?

Me: Somebody looking for momma again.

Granny: Ok.

A few days pass and the phone rings. Granny answers it this time.

Granny: Hello. She doesn't live here anymore. Ok, hold on, let me get her new number. (She sits the phone down for a few seconds and picks it back up).

Granny: You can reach her at 219-xxx-xxxx

Me: (confused) Granny. Who did they want?

Granny: Your momma.

Me: (confused look) Huh? Why did you give them that number? What number did you give them?

Granny: I gave them the phone number to the cemetery. Maybe they will get the picture now.

Me: (laughing) WOW!

I have been away from home the majority of the day. I am sitting in my car listening to music and my cell phone rings.

Me: Hello

(A voice starts speaking really fast): I need a 2 piece with some okra and a biscuit.

Me: Hello?!

(Again, the voice says really fast): I need a 2 piece with some okra and a biscuit.

Me: Wait!

The Voice: Lisa??

Me: Yes!

The Voice: Oh it's you!

Me: Granny?

The Voice/Granny: Yeah it's me!

Me: Who are you calling? Why are you talking so fast?

Granny/Voice: I thought I was calling Harold's Chicken!! I wanted to give them my order before they tried to put me on hold.

Me: Granny! Harold's Chicken doesn't deliver.

Granny: They don't!?!

Me: NO.

Granny: Aww FOOT! Well, now you know what I want. Pick it up on your way home!

PHONE CLICK

I suspect that was her plan the entire time!

We are going through a Popeyes Chicken Drive-thru. As we exit, she taps me on the shoulder and points to someone coming out of the door.

Granny: She looks like she has been eating a lot of that chicken.

In other words, she's Fat?! This is even more ironic when you consider that Granny is a "stout" woman herself.

Granny was a domestic--she was "The Help". For many years she didn't have a car or the adults in my family had to share a car. That meant she had to catch the bus to work. I remember her blue and white uniform with the belt tied in the back. My other grandma worked at a restaurant. She also wore the same kind of uniform (all white) that also tied in the back.

Although Granny didn't have a racially motivated hate towards any other group of people, she lacked finesse when communicating about other races. People are "black and white" period. No matter how many times we tried to get her to be more politically aware, she was just comfortable with what she'd heard most of her life. She even referred to food that way at times. White folks food vs. black folks food.

I have a really good friend, who happens to be white, come to our house to visit. Granny refers to her as "my white grandchild". The first time my friend visited, she got up early, and cooked some breakfast. She realized that Granny was awake and offered to get food for Granny. After some time, I noticed that Granny kept asking my friend to get things for her, even though others were around.

Me: Granny, why do you keep calling Melissa to get you stuff when the rest of us are right here?
Granny: (with a big ole smile on her face) I never had a white woman get anything for me just for asking. I am enjoying myself.

My friend Melissa found it innocently comical too. She waited on Granny hand and foot throughout her visit.

I like lots of different cuisines. I like Japanese, Greek, Italian, Mexican, Dominican...you name it. I want to try it. I also cook from various cultures. The reality is that it comes down to seasonings and cooking methods as the biggest differences, but for Granny, it's just too much.

Granny: Lisa tonight can we just be black?
Me: What does that mean?
Granny: Can you just cook something that black people eat?
Me: What does that mean?
Granny: You always cooking something I can't even say.
Me: Granny, I cook chicken, fish, beef, pork, turkey, or seafood like everybody else.
Granny: Not like black people!

Me: I just use different seasonings to give a variety of flavors.

Granny: See! I don't want all the flavors. Why can't you just use salt, pepper, and paprika?

Me: (SMH)

Me: Granny, you want me to cook some greens this weekend?

Granny: No! Cause you're gonna put turkey in them. We only use salt pork. College didn't help you. You've been messing up food ever since you went there.

Even during difficult times, she would make things funny. She had been in a rehabilitation center and had been asking to go home for days. My phone rings at 2:00 am. It is the emergency dispatch from 9-1-1.

911: Is this Lisa Bennett?

Me: Yes

911: Ms. Bennett, are you familiar with Jessie Wilson?

Me: Yes, what is going on?

911: Do you currently know where Ms. Wilson is?

Me: Yes? She is in a rehabilitation center. It is called XXXX. What is going on?

911: Ok, Ms. Bennett then don't worry. She is in fact at the facility. We had to dispatch officers to the location because Ms. Wilson notified us that she was being held against her will! We have officers on the scene who are talking with staff. We were given your information to contact.

Me: What the ???? I am on my way!!!

I am a bit confused and upset when I arrive.

Me: Granny!

Granny: (Cool as a cucumber) I told you I am ready to go home!

Me: You can't call 9-1-1 for that!!

Granny: Why? Ain't it their job to rescue people?

Me: Yes, but you are not in danger.

Granny: I didn't say anything about danger! I said, I am being HELD AGAINST MY WILL! THAT IS TRUE!

Needless to say, I had her phone removed!

My phone rings.

Nurse: Ms. Lisa, can you come to the facility? She is acting up.

Me: I am on my way, don't tell her I am coming. (I arrive & meet the nursing staff in the hallway). Can you go in there and tell her that if she doesn't take her medicine, you are going to call her grandchildren?

Nurse: Ms. Jessie, if you don't take your medicine, we are going to have to call your grandchildren.

Granny: (raised voice) What?! CALL THEM, CALL THEM! They don't run me. I raised them. Pick one. Call Lisa, Charles or Rhoda! They are my grandchildren, I am NOT theirs.

(While the nurse is standing there, I poke my head in the door.)

Me: What did you say??

Granny: Huh? (starts laughing and smiling) Nothing!

Me: Yes you did. I was standing right out there while you were clowning.

Granny: (looks at the nurse) Aww FOOT! You tricked me. That ain't fair! Just give it to me.

She takes her medicine and the drama is over.

In February 2019, our hospital stay was more than I could handle. Watching her not be able to do anything for days was so emotionally draining. This was the second time that we have found ourselves in this situation in the past 2 years. At each episode, it seems that doctors weren't sure how this was going to go. My faith was bouncing up and down. I couldn't eat, couldn't sleep. I couldn't rest at home. I needed to be with her. I couldn't focus on anything else for long. After 8 days of an emotional roller-coaster, she opened her eyes.

Granny: Michelle, where am I (that is my middle name)?
Me: You are in the hospital.
Granny: Why?
Me: You have been sick and they are trying to get you better.
Granny: Huh? Jesus is getting me better. I wanna go home and sit in my chair.
Me: You gotta stay here for a few more days then we can go home.
Granny: That's Stupid! Jesus can fix me at home. He knows my address.

I cannot tell you how WONDERFUL and AMAZING that moment felt! God heard our cries. The angels opened up the gates of heaven and poured out another blessing. As the fog starts clearing from her mind, she goes on a long litany of questions.

Granny: Lisa, while I was here, did y'all feed the dog?

She asked the question as if it was a task that she normally performs and we were subbing for her.

Granny: Where is everybody? Lisa, it's almost 11 o'clock.
It's time for some chicken. I want to eat!

The questions came as if she was never absent. She starts singing at the top of her lungs (these are the lungs that have been giving us so many problems). She is bellowing.

Granny: God is the Joy and the Strength of my Life!

By the second time through the song, the staff is coming to the room to see who is singing. They are surprised. Good news kept coming. Doctors came in one after the other and gave reports that summed up to "It is well". While we still have a way to go and Granny will never be 100% by man's measure, God was showing us favor.

I am excited, posting on social media. I want the world to know how God has given us more time. I am crying and trying to ask questions. I wanna know if she is still ok mentally. How much damage was done; what does she remember? I decided to ask basic questions to test her mental agility. I figure 3 times, with some time in between, ought to give me a baseline.

(1st Practice Session)

Me: What is your name?

Granny: Jessie Mae

Me: What is your birth date?

Granny: Oct 19, 1925 (the year is not accurate but that is another story).

Me: Can you count to 10?

Granny: Yeah, can you? (really fast and slurred she says) 1, 2,3,4,5,6,7,8,9,10!

(2nd Practice Session)

Me: Granny, what is your name?

Granny: Jessie Mae Harris

Me: No, that was your old name

Granny: Oh, yeah? I got married. It's Williams.

Me: No, it's not.

Granny: Then what is it?

Me: It's Wilson.

Granny: (hunching her shoulders) I was close enough!

(3rd Practice Session)

Me: Granny, what is your name?
Granny: (just staring at me)
Me: Granny, what is your name?
Granny: (still staring at me)
Me: (panic is starting to set in, it must be on my face) Granny:
What is wrong with you? Don't you know my name?
Me: (relieved) What is your name?
Granny: Pudding Tang! Ask me again and I'll tell you the

What do you think? I think she is on her way back!

Any day with Granny is filled with comical overture and today seems to be right in step. By this time, she has made it VERY clear that she is hungry. She has mentioned chicken several times. Make no mistake, she does NOT just want chicken, she assuredly wants FRIED chicken. Chicken prepared any other way is TRASH.

Granny: I want to eat
Me: They will test you in a while to see if you can swallow
before you can eat food.
Granny: When? I am hungry now?
Granny: (talking to her nurse) Why do you keep coming in
here without some fried chicken?

Nurse: (laughing hysterically) Can you teach me how to make
chicken and smother it with gravy?
Granny: That is easy! Ain't nothing to do, but put the flour in
the skillet, let it brown, add some onion, and black pepper.
Put the chicken in it and let it smother. If you get me out of
here, I will show you how to do it. We can make some rice
too. I can also teach you how to make oxtails, but you gotta
bring me some.

Granny did, in fact, give instructions on how to smother chicken, make neckbone soup, and oxtails before her stay was over. I am NOT going to name the staff or facility, but I offer my thanks and appreciation.

I know that Granny wants chicken for dinner. No matter what I have planned, it will never be good if it's NOT chicken. So on this day, I decided to just take one for the team. I bought her a chicken dinner with mac and cheese, yams, and greens on my way home. Now, no matter what I decide to cook for the family, she will be fine. As soon as I walk in the door, the question comes.

Granny: What are we eating?
Me: Don't worry I brought you home some chicken so you
should be fine.

She is excited and smiles. She waits patiently for me to change my clothes and prepare a plate. I sit the plate in front of her and leave the box on the counter within her reach. A few minutes later, I returned. I notice her plate is cleaned and even the box is gone.

Me: How did you eat all of that so fast?
Granny: I didn't (she points to the dog.
Sasha is licking her paws).
Me: She took your food? Sasha, get out of here!! Granny:
NO!!
Me: What happened?
Granny: I gave it to her!
Me: What did you do that for? Why did you waste my money?
Granny: Don't fuss at us. We didn't waste your money! You
wasted your money!!
Me: How? I thought you wanted chicken.
Granny: I do want chicken. I wanted FRIED chicken and you
knew that when you bought BBQ'd chicken. So this is your
fault. Now! Can you go get me some chicken?

I felt like thrashing her at that moment.

After some days in the hospital, we are progressing. The speech department has now shown up to assess her ability to swallow. They will determine what she can eat. The therapist gives her a lot of commands and she does quite well. The therapist indicates that we are going to try some "thick flavored water" first to test things.

Therapist: Ok, Ms. Wilson, let's try this and see how you do. Open now and swallow.

The therapist shows me how to verify that she is swallowing correctly. After a few minutes the therapist's leaves.

Granny: Lisa. What is this I am eating?
Me: It is some flavored water.
Granny: That doesn't taste like chicken. I don't want any more! (throws up her hand and turns away)
Me: Are you throwing your hand up at me?
Granny: Well, ain't nobody else in here but us!

My Granny was really supportive of me and, thereby, my relationships. She asked a zillion questions about being gay, sex, etc. One of her favorite shows was Law & Order.

Granny: (screaming) Lisa, Rasheida come here! Hurry!
Rasheida: (running to the room) What is wrong?
Granny: How does a woman give another woman gonorrhea in the mouth?
Us: (puzzled) What?

Granny: The lady on Law & Order got gonorrhea in the mouth! How?

Rasheida: I don't know! I never had gonorrhea.

Me: Why are you asking us?

Granny: Well, y'all put your mouths on each other, don't you? I thought you might know the answer.

She is cracking up with laughter.

Rasheida is in the kitchen. I am in my room and Granny is in her room.

Rasheida: (yells out) "Oh Shit!"

Granny: (yelling from her room) No Rasheida! Not in the kitchen! Please try to make it to the bathroom!

She is laughing hysterically.

Granny is in her room watching TV and starts screaming.

Granny: Hey. Y'all know the gay people are having a parade!? Look! They have lots of colors! You know we called them punks when I was young.

Do people call y'all punks?

Anytime Granny wants your undivided attention, she calls your name with great determination before making her statement or asking her question, even if you're alone.

Granny: Lisa! How do you fix your mouth to kiss a woman?

Me: What are you talking about?

Granny: I can't understand how you can kiss a woman?

That is weird!

Me: I just kiss the person. You are overthinking it. I am not talking to you about this.

A few hours later, I get ready to leave the house and run down the stairs towards the door to open it. Granny hears me.

Granny: You leaving?

Me: Yes. I will be back shortly.

I quickly turn and run up the stairs back towards her. I bend over and kiss her on the lips.

Me: I love you. I will see you later.

Granny: (Smiles) ok. Be careful.

As I turn to leave.

Me: Granny, now you have your answer.

Granny: What? What are you talking about?

Me: You wanted to know how I "fix my mouth to kiss a woman?"

Granny: Awww FOOT. You tricked me! That's not fair!

Granny: That's a shame.

Me: What?

Granny: The Lord blessed you with a head full of beautiful curly hair.

Me: (holding my breath) ok...?

Granny: I don't like it, but I get why you got it all knotted up (pause); 'cause you're lazy and just don't want to comb it.

Me: (scouring) Really Granny?

Granny: But why do you think boys wanna run around with their pants hanging off, their hair in knots and hanging to their ASS-HOLES?

Me: (Speechless)

Granny: They should just cut it off and look like a man. Wouldn't that be easier for them?

Me: (smh and walking away).

Granny: You and your nephews (her great grandsons) got the same hairstyle. Does that mean you want to be a boy or do they want to be girls? I think y'all all confused.

Sometimes I am not sure who is teaching whom. Granny is sittin in the car. She is waving her hands, moving her lips, and tapping her feet. I don't know what is playing on the radio, but she is jamming. I open the door and I hear:

"Bitch better have my money, Pay me what you owe me Bitch better have my (bitch better have my) Bitch better have my (bitch better have my) Bitch better have my money"

Me: *Granny, what are you listening to?*
Granny: *I like this song.*
Me: *Where did you hear it?*
Granny: *Cameron taught me.*
Granny: *(looking at me and singing) You better have my money!*

She doesn't curse, but she knows the lyrics to a Rihanna song?

When I was younger, I recall magazines that had useful household gadgets to assist the elderly. They typically had pill crushers, grabbers, etc. A few years ago, I noticed that at least one of the publications now includes "adult" toys. Granny is in her room looking through the latest edition. As she flips to the adult toy section.

Granny: *Do you have one of these? What about this one? Is this a good one? Why aren't you answering me?*
Me: *(just staring at her)*
Granny: *Well, I can't find a man at my age. If it works, I can get one.*
Me: *I am walking away!*

I am in the dining room. I can hear Granny's conversation with her aide.

Aide: I am sorry I am late Miss Jessie. I was helping a neighbor and needed to wait for an ambulance to arrive.

Granny: That's ok. You gotta help people. I hope your neighbor is ok.

Aide: I won't know till I call later, but if she takes a look at her paramedic, she will do better. He was FINE! I was stumbling over my words trying to talk to him.

Granny: Oh yeah?

Aide: Yes ma'am. I like a FINE man.

Granny: Me too. I am old, but I look. Lisa's friend, Jason, has a nice BUTT.

Me: GRANNY!

Granny: What? He knows. I told him.

My long time friend Jason stops by for a short visit.

Jason: Hey, Granny.

Granny: Hi baby!

Jason: Wait. You are looking at my butt.

Granny: Well. I am a girl and you are a boy!

Me: (laughing) Granny!

Granny: You're confused, I'm not.

My surrogate big sister, Sharifa, calls Granny, comes by to visit, and talks with Granny. She also supplies Granny with some coffee that she loves. On this day, it's nothing out of the ordinary. They catch up. At some point, Sharifa showed Granny a picture of her then fiance. A few days go by.

Granny: Lisa, have you seen her boyfriend ?

Me: Who?

Granny: The one who got the name that sounds like the "Refas", my coffee lady.

Me: Sharifa?

Granny: Yes. Her boyfriend is fine! When do you think she is bringing him over?

She also gets excited when LL Cool J takes his shirt off.

Granny: Look. Hurry up and look (She is pointing at the TV)! I bet Rasheida don't look like that without a shirt.

Granny has a few shows that she watches religiously including Jimmy Swaggart. I personally don't like the show, but that's my religious baggage. If Granny is wiggling her feet, it is well in the world. She is happy.

Me: Why do you watch him? He says some really hateful things.

Granny: I am listening to the singing.

Me: But what about the word? Does he even support black people?

Granny: Didn't you read the bible? Jesus used a jackass to preach. You ain't gotta like him. You gotta pay attention to the message. There is always something to learn.

She also doesn't remember the names of the shows or movies. She talks about the characters in Power, Law & Order, Queen of the South, and NCIS like they live next door.

She expects you to keep up when she references them. For example, "LL & the cool white boy".

Granny and I have an understanding that she shouldn't call me after 9 a.m. during the week because I am likely in a client meeting, unless it's an emergency.

My phone is ringing, so I excuse myself from a client meeting to take the call.

Me: Granny, what is wrong?

Granny: Did you see the news?

Me: What is wrong?

Granny: The purple guy! Oh my Lord, the purple guy! The Purple guy is gone!

Me: What are you talking about?

Granny: The Purple guy is gone!

Me: What purple guy? Barney?

Granny: No! The little guy that plays the guitar. Oh Lord!

Me: Prince?

Granny: Yes!!!! Oh Lord!

Me: Granny! This is NOT an emergency! What do you know about Prince?

Granny: There ain't gonna be no more Purple Rain, Purple Rain...

Me: Bye Granny!!!

Granny is watching Empire. Jamal is breaking up with his producer (boyfriend). Granny is yelling at the TV.

Granny: (screaming at the TV) He doesn't want you for a boyfriend/girlfriend anymore! Leave him alone! Lisa! How do y'all decide who is who anyway?

Now she is back to watching Empire as if she hasn't said a word. You think she is into the show?

We are watching an episode of Chicago Fire with Granny and a guy just blew up his house trying to cook "hash". She looks over at me.

Granny: (shaking her head) I don't understand!
Me: What?
Granny: How do you blow up the house cooking potatoes and onions with mashed up meats?
Me: (LMAO!) Wrong kind of hash, Granny.

Today Granny clued me in on her view of this historic event called an ECLIPSE.

Granny: I don't understand. People are always running to see what God tells us not to look at. I have been in the world for 92 years and never needed to see an eclipse.
Me: Well it only happens every few years.
Granny: But can't that make you blind or mess up your eyes?
Me: Well yes, if you look at it too long or without special glasses, but people may not get another chance to see it.
Granny: That is so stupid! You know Lot's wife turned to salt. That only happened one time.
Me: OH WOW!

Around 2011, the home occupied by my mom and grandmother burned to the ground. They were displaced in temporary housing for roughly two years during the rebuild. They had a 2 bedroom apartment with full amenities in a Residence Inn. Granny had suffered some injuries that required rehabilitation in the home. When her therapist arrived, there were a lot of people visiting. We left the apartment and went to the lounge area to give them more space and some privacy. Approximately, 30 minutes expired and the therapist asked to speak with us. He is visibly frustrated.

Therapist: I cannot get her to cooperate. I have been trying to assess her and she is being very combative. She won't do anything I ask of her.

Me: Ok. Let me go talk to her.

The therapist follows me to the room.

Me: Granny, what is wrong?

The therapist said you won't cooperate?!

Granny: Yep!

Me: Yep what? Why?

Granny: He asked me to lay on the bed.

Therapist: I have to see how you get in and out of the bed.

I need to know what you can do..

Granny: (looking at him) OH! Well, I am 90 years old. If I get in that bed and you jump on me, I can't do nothing about it! They all left. I watch the News. They rape old ladies everyday!

I am NOT getting raped!

We were all speechless. That thought never entered our minds, but she made a valid point.

Me: We're just gonna skip it today.

She isn't above asking her great grandchildren about drugs, sex, or alcohol either. My son and nephew are getting ready to go out for the evening. Just as they attempt to leave...

Granny: Hey! Y'all got some balloons? You know if you don't put a balloon on that thing, it will fall off.
Boys: (laughing) Ok. Granny, we will be safe!
Me: Really?
Granny: I need to make sure they know.

How many 20 somethings can say their great grandmother has had a "sex talk" with them?

Granny: I think your kids smoke them funny cigarettes.
Me: What are you talking about?
Granny: I know what I am smelling. I don't know how to say it good, but they are so dumb. Why don't they spray some cologne before they come into the house?

Granny: Lisa, I heard that "Refas" make you eat a lot.

Me: What? Where do you get your information? Why are you concerned about the effects of marijuana?

Granny: Well, they say you can eat it now. I wonder what would happen if we invited folks over and used it in the BBQ sauce?

Me: So you wanna get high?

Granny: I want to see what it does to other people. What do you think will happen?

Me: I don't know. I don't smoke it or eat it.

Granny: Ok. I was just checking (laughing).

I call Granny on my way home,

Me: Hey Granny. Do you need anything?

Granny: I'm good!

Me: What?

Granny: I'm good!!

Me: What the?

Granny: It means I am fine.

Me: I know what it means. Where did you get that?

Granny: The kids!

Me: What the heck are your great grandchildren teaching you?

Granny: Bye Felicia!

click: phone hangs up

I never paid attention to that strong personality trait until I got older and the roles started to reverse. She was my "provider" and "caretaker". I never questioned it, but now that the roles are reversed, I call her "stubborn". I suppose that being persistent/stubborn/determined is how you make it in this cruel world that spat on you as a kid and called you the "N" word daily. This is how you grow up and live through civil rights and the Jim Crow south. Yet with only a 3rd grade education, you purchase your own home on a "domestic's" salary. A home that you have now passed on to your children, grandchildren, and great grandchildren. Granny did whatever she needed to do. I remember her baking pies to sell for the church and for the neighborhood. She rented out rooms here and there too. But I NEVER heard her complain about money or anything. As a matter of fact, she often quotes Philippians 4:11 "Not that I speak from [any personal] need, for I have learned to be content [and self-sufficient through Christ, satisfied to the point where I am not disturbed or uneasy, regardless of my circumstances." She never worries. "In ALL thy ways TRUST/ACKNOWLEDGE God! He will direct your path! I don't worry about the Lord's business." Amazingly, upon the deaths of my mom, my aunt, and my great aunt—all within a 4 month span—she maintained.

Granny: Lisa, why are you crying?
Me: I miss my mommy
Granny: Oh (shrugs her shoulders).

Me: Granny, don't you ever miss her?

Granny: Yes, but I talk to her every day.

Me: But you never say anything or look sad.

Granny: I don't worry about God's decisions. I will just be content. He ain't gonna change his mind now. Hey, if he did and she walked in, we would run out of here anyway (laughing hard).

Me: (laughing too) I feel better now.

Me: Granny, would you please take your medicine? Granny: NO!

Me: Granny, we need you to take your medicine and eat your food. We want to take you home.

Granny: NO!

Me: You remember how you used to say that Big Mama (her mother) was getting old and stubborn?

Granny: Yep!

Me: You are acting the same way?

Granny: So you understand? Now, leave me alone!

Me: Oh boy.

Some of the fellas that grew up on my block are hanging out. I had a lot of packages to carry in the house and one of them offered to help me. We are standing in the kitchen and I am busting him up about his 1970's Superfly looking "outfit".

HE said: "You know I'm the MF real gangster in this..."

Before he could complete his thought Granny screams out from her room.

Granny: JOE BLOW, (She used his actual name) you sound like you have had too much of that stuff! Are you in the street embarrassing yourself? Go lay yourself down and sleep it off!!!

He and I were looking at each other in shock because she knew his voice. He puts his hand over his mouth like a 10 yr old who just got caught cussing and runs down the stairs and out the door. Meanwhile, Granny was calling him for a response. I was dying laughing. I ran to the door.

Me: You the gangsta, but you just got PUNKED by a 95 year old!".

Today, Granny is a bit subdued. She changed rooms and didn't really like the move. Her desire is to keep moving towards the door. She reminds us at every opportunity. She even grabbed her nurse by her uniform and said, "Baby get me outta here." She goes on to tell the nurse, "I am adopting you as my niece. Help me get out of here and I will make you some smothered chicken and rice." She is persistent when she wants something. That has always been her way.

Granny: Lisa, rub my arm. Rub it all the way down. Don't
SMASH me. I ain't dead. I can feel you hurting me. (pause)
Lisa, please call Charles or Rasheida to come get us.
I wanna go. Come on, pull my legs around so we can go.
Me: Granny we can't go, you still gotta get well.
Granny: Lord, help me! My grandchildren are full of 369.
Granny does not curse. "369" means #FOS--full of shit

Granny had an opinion on all kinds of topics, including the socially and emotionally complex issues around "me too", women's rights, and empowerment. When it came to issues around R. Kelly, Donald Trump, and others, she didn't hold her tongue. While she didn't think his behavior or that of other men was acceptable, it was a reality. Time had proven that male patriarchy is/was as ingrained in America as capitalism that led to slavery.

During the R. Kelly documentary, a few friends stopped by to hear her opinion on the topic. While others were busy debating who was at fault, she was pretty clear on her position. Her first reaction...

Granny: I think we should introduce R. Kelly to Lorena Bobbitt or we can tie him to a gurnee and shove a pencil up his pee hole and see if he likes it!!

She also thought the parents shared the blame in the victimization of their children.

Granny: When people start telling the truth, things will go a lot better. Men have been violating little girls since I was in the fields. Those would be fathers, brothers, and cousins. So when you drop off your daughter to hang out with a grown man, you should expect that all won't be well.

Granny: Lisa, you know the people that killed that baby (5 yr old AJ)? They don't need to live either. Where do we have sharks in the water? We should drop them off in it.
Me: Oh my. We should change your last name to Corleone.

Granny also loved sports. She watched Chicago Bulls & Bears games. She loved the NBA finals. She liked MJ, Kobe, and Lebron. She made it a point to watch them.

She would occasionally let a player have it. She was really mad at Kevin Love when Cleveland was playing in the finals a few years back. She blamed him for their loss.

On this particular day, James Harden caught her attention.

Granny: Why is he running around with a woman's vagina
on his face?

Me: What? Who?

Granny: They don't pay him enough money to get a good
shave?

Me: Huh? What are you talking about? James Harden makes
enough to get a shave whenever he wants too. He likes his
beard.

Granny: Well, he looks like a slave entertaining "white
folks"! No self respecting black man with money would run
around with all that hair on his face. He looks like a mess.

Me: He is no slave. He makes millions of dollars a year.

Granny: Who makes more? Him or the white man who owns
the team? If he is doing all the work and getting less, then he
is still a slave. Y'all so dumb. I bet you thought things had
changed.

I was in shock. The depth of her view had many social and economic layers that hadn't occurred to me. I was fumbling for the words to try and explain, but then I remembered that Granny was born in 1924. Her idea of a successful black man, at least in appearance, should be that of Barack Obama. No matter what I said, she was not going to agree. I just left this conversation with a lot more on my mind than basketball. By the way, although Lebron has a beard too, she likes the way he keeps it "respectable".

Granny was not sure that we made wise decisions with our money either. She had an opinion on our vehicles, clothes, and especially eating out at restaurants.

Me: Come on Granny. We're gonna go for a ride today in the convertible.

Granny: What? I didn't know you had one of those cars with no top.

Me: Yep. Let's ride.

Granny: You know. Its stupid to pay more money for a car that they already ripped the roof off.

Me: HUH

While out for a ride. Granny wants her favorite thing, some fried chicken.

Me: Granny, don't get that fried chicken grease on the seats in my car.

Granny: Are you kidding? I am not going to waste this grease.

She reaches down, pulls up her dress, and rubs her knees.

Me: OMG! (SHAKING MY HEAD)

I was blessed enough to grow up with my grandparents, great grandparents and their siblings. I sit and think about the wisdom passed on to me through the many conversations and the laughter. My eldest aunt was born in the 1890's and she was hilarious because nothing our generation did made any sense to her. Today I was listening to my 90 yr old granny and my 19 year old son having a conversation and it went something like this....

Granny: Brandon, stop eating so fast. The food is not going to run away.

Brandon: (smiling with laughter) Ok Granny

Granny: Brandon, go in my room and get that needle and thread off my dresser so I can sew up those holes. I am tired of you walking around with those ripped britches.

Brandon: (laughing so hard he is about to bust) I didn't rip them. I bought them like this. This is the style.

Granny: What? You bought them with no knees? (deep breath, pause, then loud voice) You paid money for them with holes in them already?

Brandon (laughing): Yes. I paid $100 for these jeans.

Granny: What? That's STUPID!

Brandon kisses her and gets out of the house, laughing all the way down the stairs. She still does not realize I am behind her. I get up to walk out of the room.

Granny: Hey, Lisa! Did you know your son paid $100 for those busted pants he wears?

Me (smh): Yeah. It's the style.

I am still trying to figure out how that was my fault. We laughed all day and thanked God for the GRACE & WONDERFUL BLESSINGS of our generational living arrangement! The conversations are PRICELESS!

I am laying in Granny's bed watching the game. Rasheida comes in fussing at me for not hanging up my coat. I hear her, but I turn away.

Granny: Look Rasheida! She is telling you to k-i-s-s it (kiss her butt)

Get her!"

Granny interrupted Rasheida as she was talking.

Rasheida: Granny. Are you trying to tell me to shut the hell up?

Granny: No. You didn't hear me say anything like that, but maybe you oughta listen to yourself!

Granny doesn't want to eat her food. She is mashing her lips together in protest. She and Chuck battle everyday.

Granny: I wouldn't give that to the dog. It's nasty!
Chuck: If you don't eat this food, you are never going to be able to go home.
Granny: (saying nothing. Just staring at him)
Chuck: Don't make me force YOU!
Granny: You're not my boss!
Chuck: I am today.
Granny: (after a long pause) Ok. You're the boss now?
Chuck: Open your mouth and eat.
Granny: Nope. You're the boss, but I am the BIG BOSS!

CNA: Granny said she doesn't want any more nervous pudding. What does that mean?
Me: You gotta live with her to translate. That means she doesn't want any JELLO, it shakes. She doesn't like "hen fruit" either. That means she does not want eggs.

Granny is getting stronger. We had some glimpses of her wit returning today.

Granny: Excuse me young man. (talking to a cleaning guy).
Do you all have a Coke, Pepsi, or 7up?
Me: Granny, that's not his job. He is here to clean the room.

Granny: I didn't ask him about his job! (looking at the man)

Sir, did I ask you about your job?

Cleaning guy: No ma'am.

Granny: See! I asked him for a coke. He can go back to his job after he gets me a coke!

The cleaning guy leaves without a word and returns with a bottle of coke.

Cleaning guy: Here you go Granny.

Granny: Thank you! See, his job got nothing to do with it.

Me: I guess you made your point.

By now you know that Granny says some colorful things that may NOT mean what you think they mean. We always found her choice of vocabulary to be quite amusing. Here are some of her favorite words and expressions. If you've spent any time with your grandparents or great grandparents you may have heard a few.

Stout - Means your fat

Horse is blind - menstrual cycle

Personal summer - hot flash

Wat-sa-neva - I don't care

Ear screws - earrings

Corn hole - your ass

Ninny jugs - breast

Steak street chicken - Neck bones

Hen's fruit - eggs

Under the house - in the basement

War Paint - makeup

High steppers - High heel shoes

Nervous pudding - jello

3-6-9 - you are full of shit

Pour out some water - urinate

Evening in Paris - you stink or smell bad

Under the building - in a tunnel

It's pushing - I have to pee, now

Let me heist this cat's tail - mind your business

That'stupid - anything she doesn't agree with PERIOD!

In short, my Granny was a complete character. She knew how to keep LIFE interesting. She loved and gave love authentically. Her faith was unwavering, her wit undeniable. I am grateful that I have these accounts and so many others. The lessons learned are priceless. They help me remember all of the good times and keep her close to my heart! I pray they help you remember conversations with your elders or encourage you to create memories for your family.

God's Peace and Good Journey,

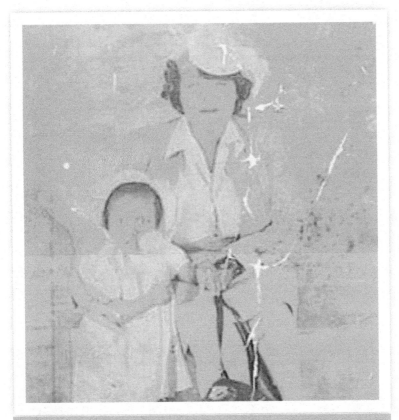

Mom and Granny

Mom and Granny

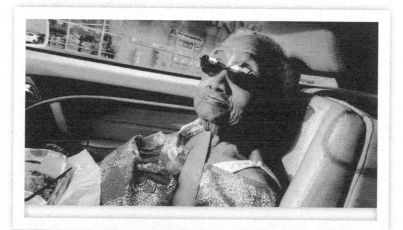

She took my shades because the sun was in her eyes...LOL

The family celebrating her birthday

I am not sure who is causing whom to misbehave

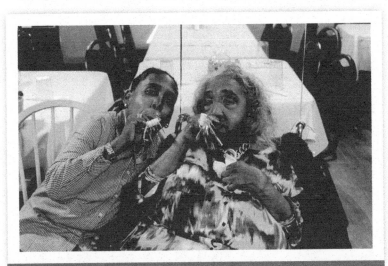

Me (her Lee- La') and Granny

Thank you

My family: Too many to list. You know who you are, you know our relationship and no one else can define your place in my life. I love you!

My FB Tribe: Thanks for asking for it and encouraging me to write it. I pray it keeps you remembering Granny and laughing when things get tough.

Team Lisa (Fearless!)

Rasheida, Chandra, Raimele, Suraj, Courtney, Daniel, Kori & Brandon. I am still looking for the correct words to express my gratitude. This would still be rolling around in my head, but you crossed every "t" and dotted every "i" to get it into the world. I THANK YOU!

Sandy S , Kathy G and Dori B. I thank God for sending you to use your gifts and talents. You helped me keep it together.

My Sheros: Kris P, Trish T, Ayana B, Dawn J, Sandra M, Cynthia J, Sharifa W, Diane C & Gladys A: When I need a gentle nudge, a kick, a push, a pull, a hug, or word of encouragement--you have been my village. Thank you for your guidance, love, and friendship.

About the Author

Lisa M. Bennett is a coach, speaker, author and Youtube personality. Formerly an executive with a multinational Global Fortune 500 consulting firm, Lisa now uses her gifts to help people gain the confidence to turn their faith into action and ideas into income.. She runs a mindset coaching practice called Fearless Coaching: "I am, I have, I can..."

Lisa credits her personal and career success to the life coaching she received from her ancestors. "When you grow up with multiple generations (great grandparents, grandparents and parents), you get the benefit of their experiences. If we just listen to 50% of the wisdom they have to share, it makes life much easier. I try to share what I have learned with others. In particular, I try to pass it on to my children and now grandchildren."

She is blessed enough to still have a multigenerational family. But instead of sitting at her elders' feet learning, she is now closer to the top with the responsibility of preserving the stories.

She has been with her love, Rasheida, for 20 years. They have 4 adult children, 12 adult godchildren and 9 grandchildren who are her world.

For more information https://linktr.ee/lmbwml